LOOK BEFORE YOU LEAP

Idioms And Phrases From Timeless Tales

Shobha Tharoor Srinivasan

Illustrations by
Sonal Gupta Vaswani

For my readers, who bring these pages to life.

Look Before You Leap
Idioms and Phrases from Timeless Tales

Shobha Tharoor Srinivasan is an award-winning voice-over artist, poet, editor and author of a dozen works of fiction and non-fiction. She is also a former non-profit development professional who spent two decades as an advocate and fundraiser for persons with disabilities. She won the Best Narration/Voice Over at the 68th National Film Awards for the film *Rhapsody of Rains: Monsoons of Kerala,* in 2022.

Shobha has published children's books in India and the United States, including the award-winning *Indi-Alphabet* (Mango and Marigold), *Prince With a Paintbrush: The Story of Raja Ravi Varma* (Westland), *It's Time to Rhyme: Poems for Kids of All Ages* (Aleph), *Parvati the Elephant's Very Important Day* (Harper Collins) and *A Treasure Trove of Timeless Tales* (Westland). Her first book for adults, *Good Innings: The Extraordinary, Ordinary Life of Lily Tharoor* (Penguin), and *A Treasure Trove of Timeless Tales* (Westland) have been translated into Malayalam.

Shobha's love of words and stories began in childhood with storytelling sessions and wordplay with her siblings. When she is not travelling in search of stories, Shobha lives in Campbell, California, with her husband. When she's not writing, doing voice-overs or multi-tasking, she can be found playing fun-grandmom to her two grandchildren, reading books, or telling tales from around the world.

RED PANDA

First published by Red Panda, an imprint of Westland Books, a division of Nasadiya Technologies Private Limited, in 2023

No. 269/2B, First Floor, 'Irai Arul', Vimalraj Street, Nethaji Nagar, Alapakkam Main Road, Maduravoyal, Chennai 600095

Westland, the Westland logo, Red Panda and the Red Panda logo are the trademarks of Nasadiya Technologies Private Limited, or its affiliates.

Copyright © Shobha Tharoor Srinivasan, 2023

Shobha Tharoor Srinivasan asserts the moral right to be identified as the author of this work.

ISBN: 9788196011840

10 9 8 7 6 5 4 3 2 1

This is a work of fiction. Names, characters, organisations, places, events and incidents are either products of the author's imagination or used fictitiously.

All rights reserved

Book design by New Media Line Creations, New Delhi

Printed at Nutech Print Services, India

No part of this book may be reproduced, or stored in a retrieval system, or transmitted in any form or by any means, electronic, mechanical, photocopying, recording, or otherwise, without express written permission of the publisher.

Contents

Introduction	vii
Don't Count Your Chickens before They Hatch	1
Dog in the Manger	4
You Can't Squeeze Blood from a Turnip	6
Necessity Is the Mother of Invention	8
A Friend in Need Is a Friend Indeed	10
Nothing Ventured, Nothing Gained	12
Look before You Leap	14
Building Castles in the Air	17
Birds of a Feather Flock Together	19
A Bird in the Hand Is Worth Two in the Bush	20
Stick Your Nose into Something	22
Honesty Is the Best Policy	24
Use Your Head	27
Slow and Steady Wins the Race	30
Bad Company	33
Snake in the Grass	35
Out of the Frying Pan into the Fire	38
Pride Comes before a Fall	40
Fish Out of Water	42
Sour Grapes	44

United We Stand, Divided We Fall	47
Sly as a Fox	49
Making a Mountain Out of a Molehill	52
Bite Off More than You Can Chew	54
Cry Wolf	56
Knowledge Is Power	59
Revenge Is a Double-Edged Sword	62
A Man is Known by the Company He Keeps	64
Like Turkeys Voting for Christmas	66
Kick a Man When He Is Down	70
The Lion's Share	72
Turn a Deaf Ear	75
As Bold as Brass	77
Add Insult to Injury	78
Caught Red-Handed	80
Better Safe than Sorry	82
Look a Gift Horse in the Mouth	84
There's No Such Thing as a Free Lunch	87
To Play With Fire	89
Quality Is Better than Quantity	90
Many Hands Make Light Work	92
Look Before You Leap	94
Author's Note	*97*
Appendix	*101*
Explore More Idioms and Phrases	*104*

Introduction

An idiom is a delightful and colourful phrase that paints a picture in your mind's eye. You cannot understand an idiom just by looking at the individual meanings of the words. The phrases are an example of figurative language, which means they add 'colour' and interest to conversation or writing but are not meant to be taken *literally*. You can't rely on the words in an idiom to tell you what the phrase means. They don't always make sense unless you are a native speaker of the language. And even then, you could come across one that leaves you scratching your head.

Mastering idioms is challenging for non-native speakers of the language but there are few other phrases that capture a culture with as much quirkiness and charm. For instance, I am sure you've heard the expression, 'It's raining cats and dogs.' This phrase is not meant to be taken literally, for it does not mean that people's pets are falling from the sky! It's a descriptive way of saying that it is raining heavily.

Idioms exist in all languages. In Hindi, they are called 'muhavre'—you may have heard your grandparents use them. In Gujarati, they are called 'kahevat'. And in Malayalam (my mother tongue), idioms are called 'bhashaprayogam'. When I was a child, my parents and grandparents used such quirky phrases all the time, so they were a big part of my childhood. I'm sure that whatever your mother tongue is, it will have similar phrases.

Some people think that idioms are odd. After all, why would we complicate things by using a phrase that does not mean what it literally says? Why say your friend was 'pulling your leg' instead of just saying that he teased you? As a teacher once told me, idioms are evidence of the fact that human beings aren't meant to function only on a literal, logical basis. Our language reflects the complex, expressive beings that we are. We choose to use descriptive phrases that paint word pictures and create funny mental images. In this way, our language and communication becomes richer and more robust—and, some might say, more human!

The English language is full of idioms. The idioms in this book have most likely arisen from the narratives that we've read in *Aesop's Fables* and the *Panchatantra*. In some cases, even if the origin of the idiom is not specifically from these classical stories, the narratives are examples of idiomatic expression.

But before we get to the stories, here are some common

phrases that are part of our everyday speech. You've probably come across at least a few of them, but you may not have known that they were called idioms.

Butter Up

To praise and flatter someone to get something out of them.
This phrase seems to come from devotees (probably in India) pouring ghee on idols while they prayed. The devotees hoped that the gods would bless them with what they wanted—usually a good harvest.

Head Over Heels

To fall hopelessly in love.
When it was first used, the words referred to the act of doing a cartwheel or a handstand. But in recent years the phrase, which describes the difficulty of this contorted and upside-down position, is used as an idiom for when you're so madly in love that you stop being careful about anything.

Apple of My Eye

Someone who is very dear and loved.
In the ninth century, it was assumed that the pupil of the eye was a round, hard object, similar to an apple. Since vision and sight are precious and prized, a person who is the 'apple' of the eye is someone very important to you.

With Flying Colours

Achieving something exceptional.

When European explorers returned home after a successful expedition, they would raise their country's flag so that people on shore saw the colours of the flag waving in the wind. The flag was an announcement of their victory.

Let the Cat Out of the Bag

To tell someone a secret.

In the sixteenth century, dishonest farmers would often hide a cat instead of a pig in a sack and attempt to sell the latter to unsuspecting customers. When the customer opened the bag, expecting to see a pig, a cat would jump out instead. The farmer would be found out and the secret would be revealed.

Turn a Blind Eye

Refusing to see something.

It is said that the British officer Admiral Nelson would often 'look' at things with his blind eye—he had no vision in his right eye—so that he could ignore a different strategic position suggested to him by his commanders in the war.

Under the Weather

To feel ill.

Sailors would go beneath the bow, the front part of the boat, whenever they felt ill. This usually protected them from storms or rain. They would literally be underneath the bad weather that could further sicken them.

Spill the Beans

To tell a secret.

This idiom most likely came from a voting process popular in Ancient Greece. People in those days voted by placing coloured beans in a vase. White beans usually meant yes and black or brown beans meant no. If someone dropped the vase and spilled the beans, the secret results of the election would be revealed in advance.

Beat Around the Bush

To avoid the main point or circle around it.

Bird hunters in Britain would spend a lot of time beating bushes to shake out the birds. This delayed the actual hunt, so the phrase came to mean avoiding the task at hand—in this case, the hunt.

Every Cloud Has a Silver Lining

Something positive in every negative situation.

Imagine that you've missed your flight back home at the end of a holiday. You may feel annoyed at first, but then you realise that you have an extra day of holiday or time with a loved one. So, despite the inconvenience, you have gained something. The phrase was first coined by the poet John Milton, in 1634, when he used the words 'silver lining' in his poem *Comus: A Mask Presented at Ludlow Castle.*

Don't Count Your Chickens Before They Hatch

A cautionary phrase against making plans that depend on something good happening before it has actually happened.

A young girl was returning home with a pail on her head after having milked some cows. She was dreaming about the future and making plans in her head. 'This good, rich milk will give me plenty of cream,' she thought. 'Then I can make some butter, which I will take to the market, and with the money I get for it, I will buy a lot of eggs for hatching. I will have a yard full of cute young chicks when the eggs hatch. Perhaps I will sell them, and with the money I get, I can buy a new dress to wear to the fair. I will look so pretty in my new dress that all the young men will look at me and try to make friends with me. I shall, of course, ignore their attention!'

As she thought of what she would wear to the fair and how she would ignore all the attention, she tossed her head smugly, and down fell the pail of milk to the ground. She looked on sadly as all the milk flowed out, and with it

Look Before You Leap: Idioms and Phrases from Timeless Tales

vanished the dream of butter, eggs, chicks and a new dress and all her pride.

Clearly no one should count their chickens before they hatch. The phrase 'don't make castles in the air' is similar in meaning.

Dog in the Manger

A person who prevents others from having something despite having no need for that item.

On a particularly warm day, a dog was wandering around, looking for a spot for his afternoon nap. He noticed an open trough, or a manger, in the shade and knew that it must be that of an ox. The manger was full of straw, which made it look like a comfortable and cozy bed. The dog jumped in and soon fell asleep.

The ox, whose manger it was, returned after a long day in the field and came to the trough to feed on some straw. Awakened from his sleep much too early, the dog stood and barked loudly. When the ox bent down for his food, he bared his teeth, and threatened to bite. Though the dog had no interest in the hay that was the ox's food, he prevented the ox from feeding. The ox had to give up his meal and walk away. He sighed and muttered under his breath, 'Some people are like the dog in the manger. He prevented me from having something that he could not have himself.

LOOK BEFORE YOU LEAP: IDIOMS AND PHRASES FROM TIMELESS TALES

You Can't Squeeze Blood from a Turnip

A person's basic nature eventually shows through disguise, no matter how much they try to be different to suit a situation.

Once, when a sage was bathing near a riverbank, he saw a kite in the air with a mouse in its mouth. The sage shouted at the bird and threw stones at it. Startled, the kite dropped the mouse on the ground.

The sage picked up the mouse, which did not seem hurt, and took it home to his wife. However, he was a little embarrassed to carry a mouse home, so he transformed it into a little girl and then led the girl home. He presented the girl to his wife and said, 'My dear wife, since we do not have any children, take care of this girl as our daughter.' The sage's wife was delighted to have a daughter finally.

Soon, the little girl grew into a beautiful young woman, and her parents began to make plans for her marriage. The sage thought his daughter was special and should be wed to someone exceptional. He thus prayed long and hard to the sun god and asked him to come and take his daughter's hand in marriage.

The sun god came down to Earth in all his fiery glory. The young woman trembled and said, 'Father, this person is unsuitable for me. I find his heat and light unbearable. Could I not marry someone else?' The sun god graciously said he would ask the wind god to meet them instead. But when she met the wind god, the young woman said to her father, 'This suitor moves fast and blows hard and is not suitable for me either.' The wind god then brought the cloud god down from the heavens. The sage was happy; his daughter again folded her hands and begged her father, 'This suitor is too stormy and stern and is not whom I wish to marry. May I have another suitor?'

Not sure what else to do, the gods said, 'Why don't we ask the mouse king to marry your daughter?' When the young woman saw the mouse king, she immediately accepted him. The sage then changed her back into her mouse state, and the wedding was conducted in a grand ceremony.

As the sage returned home after leaving his daughter to live her new life, he muttered, 'Whatever we may try to be, what is in-born can never change.'

Necessity Is the Mother of Invention

A need or problem often encourages creative efforts to solve the issue.

The idiom 'necessity is the mother of invention' is an everyday phrase these days. Did you know that it was first used in an Aesop's story?

One hot summer day, a thirsty crow flew about in search of water. She looked everywhere but could not find any water. She then noticed a pitcher under a tree and the glint of water at its base. The crow flew down and tried to put her beak into the spout of the pitcher to drink the water, but the opening was far too narrow for her beak.

She was very thirsty, so she thought long and hard. The crow had an idea. She decided to drop pebbles into the pitcher so that the water level would rise. With each pebble she dropped into the pitcher, the water began to rise. Little by little, the water reached the opening of the pitcher, and the crow was able to dip her beak in and drink to her heart's content.

She flew away happily, knowing that whenever she was in a pinch, using her mind would help. Necessity is the mother of invention.

Look Before You Leap: Idioms and Phrases from Timeless Tales

A Friend in Need Is a Friend Indeed

A true friend helps in times of trouble instead of leaving their friend alone.

A village was once destroyed by a strong earthquake. This caused the villagers to abandon their homes and leave together for another village to start life again. Though the houses in the earthquake-struck village were damaged and unsuitable for people to live in, they were more than enough for a group of mice who had lived in the village to continue living in and rear their young. Soon, the village was taken over by mice.

The village was located close to a lake. Every day, a herd of elephants passed through the village to their watering hole. Each day, as they walked through the village, the heavy elephants accidentally trampled on the many mice that would scamper about. The mice would watch in horror as their friends and family members lost their lives to the heavy feet of the travelling elephants.

The mouse chief was most upset by what was happening and summoned the courage to speak to the elephant chief.

'Dear and great animal, I come to you with a request,' he said. 'Each day, as you and your group walk to the lake, many of our mice get trampled under your feet. Would it not be possible to take a different path to the lake?'

The elephant chief was a reasonable animal, and he agreed immediately. The mouse chief was so relieved and grateful that he announced his gratitude: 'You will not regret your generosity of spirit, dear elephant. A day will come when my friends and I will be useful to you.'

The elephant chief smiled and went on his way, laughing at the possibility of the tiny mouse ever assisting him.

A few weeks later, the elephant herd was out foraging for food and got trapped in hunters' nets. Despite their size and best efforts at escaping the nets, the elephants could not break free. The elephant chief suddenly remembered the promise his small friend the mouse had made some weeks ago, so he trumpeted loudly and called out for him. The mouse came and, seeing the problem, returned to the village to bring all his friends with him.

Soon, a large army of mice waged war on the nets with their sharp teeth, which soon got shredded into pieces. The elephants unravelled themselves from the broken strings and were able to escape. The elephant chief bowed to his friend and said sincerely, 'I should have believed you, my tiny friend. Thank you for saving our lives. A friend in need is a friend indeed.'

Nothing Ventured, Nothing Gained

Success comes only by trying or taking risks.

One day, a weary hunter who had been unsuccessful on his hunt rested under a tree. He noticed a small bird on the tree was defecating and moved his position so that the droppings did not fall on his head. To his surprise, he saw that the droppings turned to gold when they hit the ground. The hunter was amazed and wanted to catch this special bird. He set a trap, and the bird, who until then had been clueless to the tricks of hunters, was caught easily. The hunter made a cage with branches and twigs and put his special bird inside it. He then began to walk home, imagining all the money he would make with this incredible find. But then he thought: 'If the king hears of my special bird with its gold droppings, I could get in trouble and lose it. It makes more sense to give the bird to the king right away.'

So, the hunter took the bird to the king and told him the wondrous tale of its gold droppings. The king was happy to own a bird with such a special talent and, thanking the hunter with a gold coin, took his gift. But the king's minister was less trusting of this story and said, 'Why would you believe this hunter and his wild imagination, Your Highness? Have you ever seen a bird whose droppings turn to gold?'

The king thought about the minister's words and agreed that it made little sense to keep this ordinary bird. He opened the cage and let the bird go. As soon as the bird escaped from the cage, he flew to a ledge of the palace walls and began to defecate. And as soon as his droppings hit the ground, they turned to lustrous gold. The king was most upset and tried to catch the bird again. But the bird, who had once been careless, had now learnt his lesson and flew far away to safety.

The king thought to himself and said, 'I should not have meekly listened to my minister; I should have been open to discoveries. Nothing ventured, nothing gained.'

Look Before You Leap

One should only embark on a difficult task after careful planning.

A fox, wandering around in the forest at dusk, missed his step and fell into a deep well. He tried to climb out but could find no means of escape. The next morning, a very thirsty goat came to the same well and peered down. Seeing the fox, he asked if the water was refreshing. The clever fox spotted an opportunity and, hiding his own distress, lavishly praised the water, saying it was cool and tasty and excellent beyond measure. 'Why don't you come down and try it?' said the fox, encouraging the goat to descend into the well.

The goat, focusing only on his thirst, jumped into the well. It was only then that the fox informed him that they would need to help each other get out of the well. 'If you place your feet on the wall and bend your head, I will climb up your back and get out, and then I will help you out as well.' The gullible goat did as was suggested and the fox leapt onto his back, held on to the goat's horns and pulled himself out of the deep well. He then began to run away.

Look Before You Leap: Idioms and Phrases from Timeless Tales

When the goat shouted out to the fox and reminded him of the promise that he had made, the fox turned around and cried out, 'You foolish old goat! If you had as many brain cells in your head as you have hairs in your beard, you would never have jumped down before you had figured out how to escape!'

The goat realised that he should have examined the situation carefully before getting into it.

Building Castles in the Air

To daydream about things that may never happen.

The phrase is similar to 'not counting your chickens before they hatch'—an idiom we found in Aesop's Fables.

There was once a miserly man who begged for alms but never shared any of his extras with the poor or needy. One day, the man was given some corn meal in addition to food. After eating his meal for the day, he took the flour, put it in a clay pot and hung it at the foot of his bed.

He went to sleep pleased that he had earned something he could use later. He lay in bed and thought, 'How lucky I am! I can sell this flour in the market tomorrow for a profit and buy some chickens with the money.' Thinking these pleasant thoughts, he fell asleep, and as he slept his dreams continued.

'Soon, I will be able to sell the eggs from the chickens, and then I can use the money I make to buy some sheep.' He smiled at the thought of his growing wealth and continued dreaming: 'And then the town nobleman will notice how rich I am and will want to give me his daughter's hand in marriage. And we will have a grand wedding, and then, a year later, my beautiful wife will give me a beautiful son.'

The man kept dreaming, but the story was not happy anymore. 'My son will be naughty and will not listen to me or his mother. I will become angry with his mother and I will push her in frustration.' As he dreamt of pushing his wife, he thrashed on the bed, and his legs kicked the pot of corn meal to the ground. All the corn flour fell to the ground and was wasted in the dirt below.

The man realised that he had been foolish and said to himself, 'I must remember not to build castles in the air.'

Birds of a Feather Flock Together

Those with similar interests or attitudes tend to form groups.

One day a flock of cranes descended on a farmer's newly seeded field with the intention of eating all the seeds. Fortunately, the farmer saw the flock land on his field and was able to cast a large net over the birds. The farmer's plan was to trap and kill all the birds so they would not destroy his crops in the future. When the farmer looked in his net, he was surprised to discover that he had captured a stork along with the cranes. The stork pleaded for his life, explaining to the farmer that he was a different and noble bird, and did not belong with the cranes. The farmer rejected the crane's arguments. 'Birds of a feather flock together. Since it was your choice to fly with the cranes, you will be treated the same as the cranes,' he said.

The stork realised that he should have been more careful with the company he kept.

A Bird in the Hand Is Worth Two in the Bush

Holding on to something rather than risk losing it to get something better.

One sunny afternoon, perched on the branch of an oak tree, a nightingale was singing away. A hawk, flying overhead saw the little bird and flew down, seizing him with her claws. The nightingale pleaded with the hawk to let him go, saying that he would sing beautiful songs for the hawk instead. The hawk laughed and said that beautiful songs would not fill her empty stomach. The nightingale pleaded again and reminded the hawk that he was not big enough to satisfy her hunger. After all, the hawk was a large bird who ought to look for bigger birds that would make for a far more filling meal.

The hawk laughed and said, 'I really would have lost my senses if I let go of a meal that is already in my hands. Why would I give up the food I already have with me to go in search of a bird and a meal that I am yet to see?'

The hawk ate the nightingale in one gulp. Sadly, everyone knows that a bird in the hand is worth two in the bush.

Look Before You Leap: Idioms and Phrases from Timeless Tales

Stick Your Nose into Something

To meddle in somebody else's business.

A merchant once started building a temple in his garden. He hired many masons and carpenters to complete this task, and they spent the day working with bricks, stones and logs of wood to erect an appropriate structure. The workers would start their work early in the morning, and when it became too hot they would take a break and eat lunch.

One day, when the workers were away, a group of monkeys spotted the garden and scrambled in to see what was going on. 'This place is like a playground,' said one monkey, picking up a hammer. As was typical of their curious nature, the monkeys grabbed things and dropped things, ran here and there, and had fun making a mess on the construction site.

One monkey noticed a large log with an object stuck in it. 'What could this possibly be?' he said to himself. 'I wonder what I can do with it.'

He did not know that the carpenter, who had been in

the middle of sawing the log when he had to leave for his lunch, had stuck a wedge of wood in the crack of the log so that the sawed crack would not close up in his absence. He had hoped the wedge would make it easier for him to resume work when he returned.

The monkey wanted to know what the object was. He pulled it this way and that, and the wedge finally came out in his hands. Unfortunately, by removing the piece of wood that was keeping it open, the long crack in the log closed and trapped the animal inside. The monkey howled loudly in pain.

The other monkeys looked at him and then at each other, and said wisely, 'It is much better not to stick our nose into something that does not concern us!'

Honesty Is the Best Policy

It is better to be honest rather than to lie, regardless of the situation or outcome.

A woodcutter was cutting down a tree at the edge of a forest. He had been working all day and was very tired. As he lifted his axe to make another stroke on the tree trunk, the axe flew out of his hands. It fell into a nearby pool and sank into its deep waters. The woodcutter was very upset. He was not a wealthy man, and the axe was essential for him to make a living. He also did not have enough money to buy another axe.

The woodcutter sat under the tree and began to weep. Suddenly, the god Mercury appeared before him and asked about what had happened. The woodcutter shared his story. Mercury immediately dove into the water and brought out an axe with a gold handle. 'Is this your axe?' Mercury asked the woodcutter.

'No,' answered the honest woodcutter, 'that is not my axe.'

Mercury placed the gold-handled axe down on the bank and went into the pool again. He came out with another axe,

Look Before You Leap: Idioms and Phrases from Timeless Tales

this one had a silver handle. The woodcutter shook his head and said that this one was not his axe either. His was an ordinary axe with a wooden handle. Mercury dove back into the pool. On his third try, he brought out the woodcutter's axe. The woodcutter was overjoyed. He said, 'Thank you, gracious Mercury. I thank you from the bottom of my heart.'

'I admire your honesty,' Mercury said. 'As a reward, I will give you all three axes. You may have the gold, the silver and your own.'

The woodcutter returned home with his treasures. Soon the entire village knew about the story and his good fortune.

There were many woodcutters in the village who were interested in making a profit. But they did not have the conscience or the honesty of the first woodcutter. One by one they ran to the forest, hid their axes, and wept and wailed, asking for Mercury's assistance. Mercury soon appeared, first before one woodcutter, then another. With each one he brought out an axe of gold, but when they reached for the axe, claiming it was theirs, he gave them a hard whack on the head with the axe and sent them home.

All the woodcutters swiftly learnt that honesty is the best policy.

Use Your Head

To use your own intelligence to think logically and rationally.

One day, an old and tired heron sat by the banks of a lake and wondered how he could feast upon the fish of the lake without using too much effort. He did not have the strength of his youth and had become quite thin and hungry. He decided that coming up with a crafty plan that made his task easier was the best way to go.

The heron suddenly began to cry loudly.

A kind crab popped his head out of the water and asked, 'Uncle, why are you weeping? What makes you so sad?'

Wiping his tears, the heron replied, 'My dear friend, I weep knowing what I now know. I just overheard some fishermen say that they planned to drain this lake soon and take all the fish in its waters. I am so very sad to know that you will all lose your lives, and that is why I am crying.'

'This is terrible news,' said the crab. 'I must let the others know.' He dove beneath the surface of the water to tell the fish what he had heard.

Soon there was a loud clamour of anguish. All the fish swam to the top of the lake and started calling out, 'Dear Uncle Heron, you must do something to help us. You are tall and capable. Please tell us what to do.'

The heron stood up brightly and said that he knew of a large lake not so far from this one and perhaps he could transport the fish one by one on his back. The fish were all willing and hurried out of the water for their journey.

The heron, of course, had no intention of taking the fish to any other lake. As soon as he moved a little away from this lake with the fish on his back, he stopped and dashed the fish against a big rock and made a meal of it. No one knew of this dastardly plan so he kept coming back to transport willing travellers!

Soon it was the crab's turn. The crab climbed eagerly onto the heron's back and prepared for his new life. As they flew towards the lake, the crab looked down. He noticed a huge heap of fish skeletons and bones close to a large rock below. He now knew what awaited him, but he did not panic. In his friendliest voice, he said, 'Uncle, you must be tired. Shall we stop a while?'

The heron flew down to the ground and as he did, he said, 'Yes I am stopping, as I plan to crush your head against the rock below and make a meal of you soon.'

As soon as he heard these words, the crab used his sharp claws to grip the heron's neck and strangle him to death.

After his fortunate escape, the crab thought, 'When things become difficult, don't lose heart. Use your head and make a new start!'

Slow and Steady Wins the Race

Making consistent and focused effort, even if it takes time, eventually leads to success.

There once was a speedy hare who was always boasting about how fast he could run. Tired of hearing him show off, a tortoise challenged him to a race. Looking at the slow movements of the tortoise, the hare laughed loudly and agreed. The other animals in the forest were equally tired of the hare. They gathered to watch the race.

The hare and the tortoise got ready for the race. One of the squirrels waved a chequered flag and the hare took off, running down the road. Looking back, he noticed that the tortoise was slowly shuffling along. The hare cried out, 'How do you expect to win this race when you're walking along at your slow, slow pace?' The tortoise didn't reply. He kept on moving forward.

The hare was so far ahead that he decided to take a break and rest. He stretched out on the side of the road and fell asleep. He thought he had plenty of time. Meanwhile

LOOK BEFORE YOU LEAP: IDIOMS AND PHRASES FROM TIMELESS TALES

the tortoise kept walking and went on to pass the napping hare. He was now close to the finish line. The animals who were watching whooped loudly in support. Their cheers woke up the hare. He jumped up with a start and began to run again, but it was too late to catch up—the tortoise had already crossed the finish line.

The animals called out to the hare: 'Don't brag about your lightning pace, for slow and steady won the race!'

Bad Company

Unpleasant people who could be a bad influence.

There was once a white flea, who lived in the bedroom of a king and spent his days feasting on royal blood. The flea was, however, a considerate soul and was careful to only dine on the king's blood when he was asleep.

One day a bug entered the room. The flea noticed the bug and asked him to leave. 'You are a nuisance in the royal chambers and could be an irritation to the king if you were to touch his skin. Please leave us and this room immediately,' he said.

The bug was unmoved. 'This is not the way to treat a guest. You are meant to make me feel welcome. I have never tasted royal blood. The king probably dines on the choicest of foods and his blood must be very tasty. You must let me remain and share your bounty with you.'

The flea was a gentle and polite soul and did not know how to refuse his guest, so he said, 'You may remain if you like but you must promise to only feast on the king after he is asleep so that he does not feel the disturbance of your bite.' The bug agreed, but as soon as the king entered the chamber, he forgot his promise, lost his patience, and sat on the king's royal arm to take a bite.

The king howled in pain and immediately called his guards, shouting, 'There is a bug in this room!' Waving sticks, the guards rushed in to catch the culprit, but the bug immediately hid himself in a corner of the room. It was only the poor flea who was found between the sheets. The guards swiftly beat the flea to death.

With his dying breath, the flea gasped, 'What a fool I have been. It is so very important to keep away from bad company!'

SNAKE IN THE GRASS

An unfaithful friend who pretends to be loyal to you.

There was once an old sage who lived in the temple grounds of a village. He was respected and loved by the village dwellers, who sought his advice and blessings for important matters. Every time a villager came to see the sage, they brought gifts and money for the wise man. He sold the gifts, that the sage did not require, in the market and converted them into coins.

Soon the sage was a very wealthy man. But the more money he accumulated, the more worried the sage became. 'I am sure people are going to try to steal my wealth,' he thought. He put all his coins into a pouch and then slung the pouch over his shoulder. 'Now, no one can steal my money without taking it off my body,' he said to himself, 'and I will never let that happen.'

A thief who was passing by noticed that the simply dressed sage had a heavy bag over his shoulder. He watched him from afar for a few days. The thief thought, 'I'm sure there is something valuable in the pouch that the sage is wearing. The old man never takes it off. I will not be surprised if he even sleeps wearing the bag.'

The thief was determined to take the sage's money, but he knew that he would have to trick the old man. Being a shrewd and cunning thief, he made a plan. He went to the sage, fell at his feet and said, 'Oh great and wise guru, I am tired of this life of getting and spending. I need to learn of spiritual and noble matters, and I would like you to take me as your disciple and teach me the wisdom that you have gained so that I can live a better life until the end of my years.' The sage was touched by the stranger's words, and he immediately accepted him as a disciple but with the condition that the man would not be allowed to reside in the temple at night.

The thief began his studies under his guru, the sage. He was a steady and earnest disciple, and attended to the old man's daily needs with respect. The thief was hoping to win the sage's trust, but he noticed that the bag remained on the old man's body day and night. Just when the thief was about to give up and make a new plan, a young boy from the next village came to the sage and invited him to his home to conduct an auspicious ceremony. The sage agreed.

'This is my chance to rob the old man,' thought the thief. Pleased at the possibility, he set out with his guru on a journey to the next village. Much to the thief's disappointment, the sage never asked him to carry his bag. Though he struggled under the weight of it, he shuffled on, making sure the bag remained on his body and the thief at his side. Then they came to a river, where the sage said that he needed to bathe. Removing his cloak and wrapping the bag in it, he called the thief and said, here, hold my cloak so that it does not get wet. I will return soon.'

As soon as the sage turned his back to him, the thief dropped the cloak and ran off with the pouch full of money. When the sage returned after his bath, he saw that he had been swindled and all his money had been stolen.

'Oh, what a fool I've been,' said the sage. 'I should have known that wealth would be a source of trouble for me. I should have known not to be taken in by the sweet words and flattery of a crook. He was a snake in the grass all along.'

Out of the Frying Pan into the Fire

To escape a bad or difficult situation only to end up in one that is even worse.

One day a stag was wandering about in the forest, when a hunter's hounds began to chase him. Afraid of being attacked by the dogs or shot by the hunter, the stag ran into a cave for shelter. He hoped that the cave would be a refuge and a safe place from his pursuers. Unfortunately, a lion was taking shelter in the cave. When he stepped out of the shadows the stag became easy prey.

'How unfortunate I am,' cried the stag. 'I saved myself from the menacing dogs only to fall into the clutches of a lion. I have gone out of the frying pan and into the fire!'

Look Before You Leap: Idioms and Phrases from Timeless Tales

Pride Comes before a Fall

To think too much of yourself without humility and grace could lead to harmful outcomes.

Two cockerels found themselves in the same farmyard and began to fight. Both wanted to be the bird in charge of the place. The fight went on for some time, but eventually one cockerel emerged as the victor. The one who was defeated went to a corner of the yard to lick his wounds and hide. The cockerel who won crowed loudly, flapped his wings and twirled in a celebratory dance.

He then pranced around the yard, showing the others that he had won the fight and was in charge of the farmyard. Just then, an eagle that was flying above saw the parading cockerel and swooped down. He caught the bird and carried him off. The cockerel who until then had been hiding, came out of his corner of the yard and took charge. As his rival was no more he was able to rule the yard as he wanted.

The other chickens in the yard shook their heads and clucked, 'Pride comes before a fall.'

Look Before You Leap: Idioms and Phrases from Timeless Tales

Fish Out of Water

To feel awkward or unhappy because of a situation, or surroundings that are unfamiliar.

A lion and a lioness lived a happy life in the jungle. They spent their days roaming and hunting together, but when the lioness gave birth to two lion cubs, the task of hunting and finding food became the lion's job.

Every day the lion would go out to hunt and bring something back for the lioness and the cubs. On one occasion, he hunted near and far but found nothing to kill. As he was returning home, he came across a baby jackal who had been separated from his pack. The lion picked up the baby jackal, looked him in the eye, but couldn't bring himself to kill him. He brought the jackal home to his wife and two cubs and offered him as a meal.

'How can I kill an infant you have spared?' said the lioness. 'I will raise this small jackal as a cub of my own. He can play and grow with our sons and be a part of the family.' The lion agreed, and the jackal became a beloved member of the family, receiving the same love and affection that the lion cubs received.

One day, the three cubs were playing, when they saw a wild elephant. The lion cubs immediately advanced towards the elephant, but the little jackal said, 'Brothers, the elephant is our enemy and can hurt us. Let us retreat before we are hurt.' The lion cubs were persuaded to leave, but they were annoyed. It was in their blood to fight elephants, and they laughed at their jackal brother and called him a coward for his words of caution.

The jackal went to his mother, the lioness, and said, 'Mother, my brothers have disrespected me and been very rude to me. I am no less than them in intellect or status, but they call me a coward. I have come to let you know that I will take my revenge on them.'

Letting out a mighty roar, the lioness said, 'Though you were adopted by our family, you are not a lion, even if you were raised as one. Your habits and instincts are of another species, and now that you are older, those instincts are becoming clear. You should leave before my cubs turn on you. Go find your own kind.'

The jackal realised the gravity of her words and left to find the other jackals in the jungle. He knew then that it was important to know the truth about yourself and act accordingly. All this time, while with the lions, he had been a fish out of water.

Sour Grapes

To have a poor attitude towards something because it cannot be acquired.

One day, a hungry fox was wandering around in search of food. He came across a farmer's garden and spotted a beautiful bunch of ripe grapes hanging from a vine. The grapes looked large and luscious and bursting with juice. The fox's mouth watered as he imagined eating the delicious fruit. He gazed longingly at the bunch of grapes but realised that the grapes were high and out of reach.

The fox decided that if he jumped, he could grab the hanging fruit with his mouth. The fox jumped high but missed the target on his first attempt. He then walked a short distance and ran towards the fruit, jumping higher this time, but sadly fell short again. Again, and again, the fox jumped, but each time he failed to grab the grapes.

The fox sat down with a sigh and looked at the grapes. 'What a fool I am,' he said. 'I can tell that these grapes aren't

Look Before You Leap: Idioms and Phrases from Timeless Tales

good. I'm sure they're unripe and sour. Why am I wearing myself out for a bunch of sour grapes?' He then walked off scornfully, insisting that the grapes, which only a few minutes ago had been delicious, were actually inedible.

United We Stand, Divided We Fall

It is more fruitful to stick together and work in collaboration with others instead of working against each other.

One sunny day a flock of birds was flying together in the sky. Suddenly, one of the birds noticed some grains on the ground. 'Grain! Plenty of grain here,' said the bird. 'Let us land. I'm hungry and tired. Are the rest of you?'

The leader of the birds was wise, and he cautioned his flock. 'We should not act in haste. The scattered grain could well be a trap to catch us.'

'I see no danger,' said a young bird.

'I agree. Those grains look delicious,' said another.

But the leader of the birds was right. Hiding in a bush was a hunter with a net. 'I hope those silly birds come down soon,' he thought.

As soon as the birds landed, the hunter threw his net over them. The birds panicked. They flapped their wings and tried flying in different directions. Some flew left. Some flew right. But unfortunately, the net had covered them so well that there was no escape.

'We should have listened to your wise words,' they said to their leader.

Their wise leader remained calm. 'We can still escape. Stop trying to fly in different directions. If all of us fly in one direction, we have a better chance of getting away. On the count of three, let's all fly this way,' he said, pointing. 'One, two, three!'

The birds took off together, taking the net with them. The hunter watched them fly away. 'I lost not only my catch but also my net!' he cried.

The birds landed near a pond where they had friends—the mice. 'Dear friends, we need your help,' said the leader of the birds. The mice bit the net into pieces with their sharp teeth. The birds flew away happily. By banding together, the birds had defeated their enemy. They remembered, 'United we stand, divided we fall.'

Sly as a Fox

To be crafty, cunning or dishonest.

Two crows made their home in a big banyan tree. They were happy there until they decided to have some baby crows. They soon learnt that there was a big black snake that lived in the hollow of their tree, and he was particularly fond of crow eggs. Every time Mother Crow laid some eggs, the black snake would slither out and eat them all. Not even one egg had the chance to hatch into a baby crow.

The Mother Crow was very sad. She said to her husband, 'We cannot carry on like this. We must move as far away from this horrible snake as soon as possible. We do not have the strength or the skills to prevent this greedy reptile from eating our offspring.'

Father Crow was reluctant to agree. He calmly said, 'We made our home here so many months ago, and we have been so happy in these wonderful surroundings. How can we now fly to someplace new and start our life all over again?'

Mother Crow tried to feel hopeful like her husband and agreed to lay a few more eggs. But the black snake slithered out again and ate all the eggs. The snake did not even spare one egg.

Mother Crow was heartbroken. She flapped her wings and cried out, 'This must end. I cannot witness this massacre and do nothing about it.' She turned to her husband and said, 'You MUST do something. We have to find a way to stop the black snake.'

Father Crow agreed that it was time to seek help. He knew that his friend the jackal was wise and capable of helping out—and he was right. The jackal immediately reassured Father Crow. 'Why are you so worried, my friend? I know you think you cannot stop this slimy snake, but listen to my plan and you should have a large brood of baby crows in no time! Here's what you do. Ask your wife to fly to the nearby palace and steal something precious from there. She needs to make sure that the security guards at the palace notice the theft.' He then whispered more instructions to Father Crow.

The next day, Mother Crow flew to the palace. She saw that the princess was bathing in the royal baths and had removed her ornaments and left them on the bank of the river. Mother Crow slowly circled, made sure that she was in view of the palace guards, swooped down and grabbed a glittering necklace in her beak.

She began to fly away slowly, checking now and again that the guards were in pursuit. When she reached the banyan tree, she immediately dropped the necklace into the hollow of the tree, where she knew the black snake lay coiled. The glimmer of the shiny necklace glowing in the sunlight brought the snake out. The guards immediately pounced on him and beat him to a hasty death.

Father Crow smiled with satisfaction and said, 'Remember this – even stronger and more powerful enemies can be overcome with cunning. When one is as sly as a fox, even the powerful can be outwitted.'

Making a Mountain Out of a Molehill

To make a big fuss about something very small.

There was once a village, over which loomed a mountain that the people of the village cared deeply about. One day, the people of the village noticed that the mountain was in a state of stress. Smoke was coming out of its summit, the earth beneath it was quaking and trees and boulders were tumbling everywhere. The villagers were sure that something horrible was going to happen. They all gathered in fright, waiting with bated breath.

Suddenly there was a violent earthquake and the side of the mountain opened up to reveal a deep crack. The people fell to their knees, praying. A small mouse poked his little head through this crack in the mountainside. He then came running towards the worried villagers.

The villagers realised it was a situation they could not do anything about. 'We just made a mountain out of a molehill', someone said, chuckling.

LOOK BEFORE YOU LEAP: IDIOMS AND PHRASES FROM TIMELESS TALES

Bite Off More than You Can Chew

To agree to do more than you actually can.

The phrase dates back to the 1800s in America, where it was common practice to chew tobacco. People would offer others a bite of their tobacco block, and some would greedily take a bite bigger than they could chew. People began to notice and started warning others not to bite off more than they could chew.

A long time ago, a wealthy villager who wished to protect his wealth from thieves and bandits buried a huge lump of gold in a rice field. Many years later, a farmer who was ploughing the field felt his plough hit something in the ground. He stopped the plough to examine what the object was, thinking it must be an old tree trunk or the carcass of an animal. To his surprise, he unearthed a large lump of gold. Since it was broad daylight, he decided to cover up the treasure and return at night to take what he had found. He wanted nobody in the village to see what he was carrying home.

At night the farmer returned to the same field and

attempted to pull out the lump of gold. But it was so huge that he did not have the strength to lift it. He tied a rope around the lump and attempted to hoist it, but it refused to budge. The farmer was frustrated—he had found treasure that would make him wealthy, but he did not have the strength to pull it out of the ground! He was a simple man, and his approach to everything was sincere. The farmer decided to break up the lump into four portions so that each portion could be pulled out of the ground. In this way he could carry the gold home one piece at a time.

He said to himself, 'Let me not bite off more than I can chew. I will use one lump to take care of my family's daily needs, I will save one piece for a rainy day, I will one piece invest in the farm so that it benefits others in the future and one piece I will share with the poor and the needy.'

And with this wise decision, he was able to unearth the gold and live a happy life.

CRY WOLF

To call for help when help is not actually needed or raising a false alarm.

There once was a young shepherd who tended his sheep at the foot of a tall mountain near a dark forest. He would take his flock to graze every day. His was a lonely job and the boy began to get bored with his task. He needed some excitement. So, one day, he thought of a plan to get himself some company.

The young shepherd left his sheep to graze at a distance from where he could spot them. Then, he rushed down towards the village, calling out, 'Wolf! Wolf!' Hearing his cries of alarm, the villagers came running to help. They spent all day with the shepherd as they searched for the wolf, so he did not feel alone or scared.

Happy that his plan had been successful, the young shepherd tried the trick again a few days later. 'Wolf! Wolf!' he cried once again. Once again, the villagers rushed to his side, but, once again, no wolf was found.

A few days later, as the boy was looking after his sheep, a wolf emerged out of the dark forest to hunt the flock.

Look Before You Leap: Idioms and Phrases from Timeless Tales

The boy raised a loud alarm immediately, but this time the villagers, who had been fooled twice before, thought the boy was deceiving them again. Nobody bothered to come to his side. and the boy lost his entire flock

When the boy returned, weeping and complaining about the loss of his sheep, the villagers said, 'You cried wolf too many times. A liar will not be believed, even when he speaks the truth.'

KNOWLEDGE IS POWER

Knowledge provides a person with insight and resources that make them powerful.

Once upon a time, in a dense and large forest, there lived a strong and powerful lion. But he was also a greedy beast, and he destroyed all the animals in the forest either for sport or for food.

The animals thought, 'Soon we will all be wiped out.' They decided it was time to do something about the lion if they wanted to survive.

The most courageous among them came together and went to the lion. 'Oh mighty lion, great king of the forest, we know that you are stronger than us and can easily catch any of us for your meal,' they said. 'But we have a suggestion that should make you happy. We are a reasonable group of animals. Will you please hear us out?'

'What do you want from me?' roared the lion.

'What if we offered you one of us as your meal each day? You would not have to hunt for your dinner. Your meal would come right to you,' they responded.

The lion thought about it. 'What could go wrong with such a plan? I am assured of my daily meal and I will not have to work for it! This is even better than going on a hunt each day for my nourishment.' He accepted the animals' offer and went back to laze in the sunshine near his den.

The animals gathered and made a list of names so that each day one name could be drawn. The animal whose name was drawn would be sent as a sacrifice to the lion. Each day one name was drawn from the list and an animal went on their sorry way. This went on for a few days. The lion did not have any complaints. Then came the hare's turn.

Now the hare was a smart animal, and he thought aloud, 'There must be something I can do to save myself.' He devised a plan and set out slowly to meet the lion.

The lion was accustomed to a timely delivery, so he was furious when he saw the hare approaching much later than his appointed time. 'Not only are you late for my dinner,' roared the lion, 'but you are also a pathetic and small creature who will barely serve as the first course of my meal. I am going to eat you and then, as punishment, I will go to the animals and eat them all one by one!'

The hare bowed low and said in a quivering voice, 'O mighty lion, please listen to my story before you eat me or wreak havoc on the forest. Five of us had been sent to you since I am, as you say, a pathetic, small animal. But on our way here, we were pounced on by a large and ferocious lion that ate the other four animals in one swift bite. In fact, I barely escaped with my life, and that is why I am so late.'

The lion was surprised. 'What do you mean another, more powerful lion? How is that possible? Take me to him at once and I will show him that I am the king of this jungle.'

The hare walked ahead and led the lion to a well that he had crossed on his way. The lion peered into the well and saw his reflection, which he mistook for another lion. He roared to show his strength, but from the bottom of the well a louder and deeper roar echoed back. He snarled and bared his teeth, but the lion in the well exposed his canines as well. The lion was so angered by this behaviour that he jumped into the well to attack his enemy. But, of course, he drowned in the deep waters of the well.

The hare skipped back to the other animals, alive and triumphant at the success of his clever plan. From then on, all the animals lived happily ever after. They had learnt that knowledge is power.

REVENGE IS A DOUBLE-EDGED SWORD

Seeking revenge harms both those who take revenge and those against whom it is taken.

There was once a farmer who was a very hardworking man. One morning he discovered that a fox had slipped into his yard and stolen his chickens the previous night.

He was devastated and determined to lay a trap and catch the thief. Soon enough, the fox was trapped farmer doused a rag in fuel, tied it to the fox's tail and set the tail on fire.

Unfortunately, the fox, howling in pain, ran all over the place and ran into the farmer's fields. The fields were full of corn that was standing ripe and ready for picking. As the fox ran, his burning tail set the ripe corn stalks on fire. Soon the fields were completely burnt to ashes.

The farmer stared in grief at his lost harvest. While taking revenge may have felt good at first, the farmer soon realised that there were negative outcomes associated with his quest to punish the fox. He said, 'Indeed, revenge is a double-edged sword!'

Look Before You Leap: Idioms and Phrases from Timeless Tales

A Man is Known by the Company He Keeps

Those who associate with fools are often thought to be fools themselves, while those who surround themselves with wise people are considered wise.

One day a farmer got the opportunity to take in a donkey on a trial basis.

When the farmer arrived at his farm, he released his new donkey into the pasture with the other animals. Sadly, the farmer noticed that the new donkey immediately went towards the laziest donkey in the herd and began to graze by his side.

The farmer immediately returned the new donkey to the seller and said, 'This ass is as worthless as his choice of companion. I know a man by the company he keeps.'

LOOK BEFORE YOU LEAP: IDIOMS AND PHRASES FROM TIMELESS TALES

LIKE TURKEYS VOTING FOR CHRISTMAS

To seek a situation that is sure to have a negative outcome.

Turkeys are often the favourite choice of food for Christmas dinner in the western world. When people accept a decision which is not going to work out well for them it is like turkeys voting for Christmas.

A lion lived in the forest with his friends the leopard, the jackal and the crow. Together they searched for and found prey, and the lion usually made the kill that they then shared together. With this arrangement and their close friendship, they were a well-fed and happy group.

One day, during their hunt, they saw a camel grazing on a patch of grass in the distance. 'What is this tall and strange-looking animal?' asked the lion. 'Is he of the forest or from some village? I have never seen a creature like this before.' His friends chimed in, 'This is a camel, dear friend. He is large and well-fed and will make a tasty meal for all of us for a long time.'

The lion roared in displeasure. 'What a mean-spirited remark that is, my friends. This animal is a guest in our habitat. We have a duty to make him feel at home. Go over to this camel, assure him of his safety and bring him to me.'

The jackal, the leopard and the crow went immediately to do the lion's bidding and brought the camel, who they discovered had been separated from his caravan, back with them to the lion.

'You are welcome here, dear camel,' said the lion. 'Why would you wish to return to your group and be a beast of burden again? Stay with us in the jungle and enjoy your freedom and the abundant grass and foliage here.' The camel agreed to stay and the group lived happily for a while.

Then one day, the lion got attacked by a mad elephant and was seriously injured by the elephant's tusk. The lion was in pain and unable to hunt, which meant that his friends also had no food. For many days the animals went without anything to eat. Finally, the lion called the jackal, the leopard and the crow to his side and said, 'Go find some food for all of us soon, or we will all die of hunger.'

The trio of hunters went to find food, but after a long search returned empty-handed. The jackal said to the lion, 'We have searched in vain all over the jungle and found nothing substantial to eat. But there is, after all, a large animal right here who could easily feed us for a long time. Why don't we just kill the camel and eat him?'

Tired and hungry though he was, the lion reminded his friends of the promise they had made to the camel. He was unwilling to break that promise.

Dejected by this decision, the jackal asked, 'If the camel were to willingly offer himself in sacrifice, would you then make a meal of him?' The lion smiled and nodded.

Soon the animals gathered in front of the lion. The crow first offered himself. 'Dear lion, we are all famished but there is no food in the forest. Why don't you eat me, small though I am, and at least satisfy a small part of your hunger?'

The lion smiled at his friend but shook his head and turned him down.

The jackal then spoke up. 'Lion, it would be an honour for me to give myself to you. In fact, if I should feed your hunger, I will be blessed in the afterlife, and for this noble deed, I will be welcomed in heaven.'

The lion shook his head and turned down the jackal's offer as well.

Then the leopard stepped ahead and said, 'Dear lion, I am a larger animal and your dearest friend. If you make a meal of me, your hunger will be satisfied for some time. Please consider me your next meal.'

The lion smiled feebly but said an emphatic, 'No.'

The camel had watched all this. He thought, 'I may not be an old friend, but I have been treated well here so I must make an offer as well. Since the lion has turned down all the previous offers, I'm sure that he will not make a meal of me.'

Kneeling before the lion, he said, 'Dear friend, I have enjoyed your warmth for some time, and since it is now your hour of need, I wish to offer myself to you as a gift to satisfy your hunger.'

As soon as the words left the camel's mouth, all four animals jumped on the camel and took him up on his offer.

With his dying breath, the camel thought, 'I should have known never to trust the sweet words of a devious group.'

Kick a Man When He Is Down

To hurt or insult a person when they are at their weakest.

One day a fox who was wandering around in a forest came upon a pack of dogs chewing on the carcass of a dead lion. The dogs were gleefully tearing at the skin of the lion with their teeth. The fox stopped and looked at the dogs. 'If this lion had been alive, you would have noticed that his claws are much sharper than your teeth,' she said. 'It is much easier to kick a man when he's down.'

Look Before You Leap: Idioms and Phrases from Timeless Tales

The Lion's Share

The biggest portion.

Many years ago, a lion, a fox, a jackal and a wolf decided that they would hunt together. They agreed that they would share with each other whatever they caught and killed.

One day the wolf saw a stag and was able to capture it on his own. He immediately called his hunting comrades to share his prey. The team gathered, and, without being asked to, the lion took charge and placed himself at the head of the dead stag to carve out the shares. The lion began dividing the spoils with a great display of fairness as he started to count the guests who would feast.

'One,' he said, counting on his claws. 'That is me. Two. That's the wolf. Three is the jackal. And the fox makes four.' He carefully divided the stag into four equal parts. 'I am the king of the jungle,' he said when he had finished his carving, 'so I will get the first part.' The lion then looked at the second piece, what the wolf thought would be his, and said, 'This next part falls to me because I am the strongest.'

Look Before You Leap: Idioms and Phrases from Timeless Tales

The lion then looked at the third piece that he had set aside for the jackal and said, 'this piece is mine because I am the bravest.'

His hunting partners drew closer in shock, but the lion stood tall and glared at the others savagely. 'If any of you have any claim to the part that is left,' he growled looking at the fox who had hoped the fourth piece was his, 'now is the time to speak.'

The lion's share was indeed the largest.

Turn a Deaf Ear

To ignore all advice or requests.

There was once a turtle who lived a happy life in a lake with two swans, who were his friends. They passed their days cheerfully until they noticed that the lake was getting smaller and smaller every day—the water seemed to be drying up. Worried, one of the swans said, 'If the waters of this lake dry up, we will not be able to find food and then all three of us will perish.'

The turtle thought long and hard and came up with a plan. 'Fly some distance, my friends, and search for another lake that we can all move to. We can make our new home there.' The swans agreed and flew away. When they returned, it was with the good news that they had found a perfect lake to call home.

The turtle then began to search for a long stick. Finally, after finding one, he told his friends that he would grip the centre of the stick with his mouth while each swan could grab an end of the stick in their beak. This way, they could fly with the turtle to the new lake. The swans were worried about this dangerous plan. They cautioned the turtle to be careful during the flight and to not open his mouth while they were up in the air.

The journey was going well until the turtle decided to look down. He noticed a crowded and lively village below them. He was so excited by the colourful scene that he opened his mouth to comment on it, but as soon as he did, he fell to the ground.

Since he had foolishly turned a deaf ear to his well-meaning friends' advice, he had come to a sorry end.

As Bold as Brass

To be very confident, sometimes to the point of being conceited.

Once a hungry jackal was walking through the forest in search of food when he heard a very disturbing sound. 'Oh my God, what is this deep, booming noise? Perhaps it is some large and fierce animal that is looking for food. If it finds me, it will surely make a meal of me.' Frightened and worried, the jackal decided to flee the scene. But as he turned, a more courageous part of him said, 'Why should I run away without knowing the cause of the sound? Perhaps it is nothing to be afraid of after all.'

The jackal walked towards the sound and found himself on an abandoned battlefield. In the middle of the field was a large war drum resting near a tall tree. Every time the wind blew it rustled the tree's branches, which brushed against the drum and caused a deep sound.

'There is no animal here, and there is no threat to be afraid of,' said the jackal, laughing. He walked up to the drum and bravely beat a sound on both sides of it. As he walked on in search of food, he called out confidently, 'It pays to be as bold as brass. The brave succeed.'

Add Insult to Injury

To make a bad situation worse.

One day a bald man sat down to rest after a long day of work. A fly that was trapped in the room flew around the man and landed on his head. The bald man was annoyed and tried to shoo the fly away, but it kept coming back. The man got out a stick and attempted to smack the fly. Sadly, he smacked his own head instead.

The fly laughed and said, 'Instead of insulting me, you have injured yourself. Now tell me, who is the bigger fool? You have added insult to injury!'

LOOK BEFORE YOU LEAP: IDIOMS AND PHRASES FROM TIMELESS TALES

Caught Red-Handed

To get caught while doing something wrong or illegal.

Once upon a time, a jackal, who was in search of food, wandered into a village. As he entered the village, he was spotted by the village dogs, who immediately began to chase him. The jackal ran blindly to escape the snarling dogs and fell into a vat of dye in a washerwoman's home. When he managed to get out of the vat, he noticed that he had turned completely blue. However, interestingly, the once advancing dogs were now retreating and running away from him.

The jackal was curious about this behaviour. He slowly made his way back to the jungle to see what would happen. There, as well, he noticed that all the animals were frightened by his strange appearance and backed away. The cunning jackal immediately thought of a plan. He announced in a deep voice, 'Dear animals, do not be afraid. I have been sent by Lord Brahma as a protector of the forest. My purpose is to look after you.' The animals bowed to him with gratitude and said, 'O divine and unusual creature, we are at your command. We will, from now on, take care of you forever.'

The first thing that the blue jackal did was banish all the other jackals from the forest, in case they recognised him as a jackal under his blue fur. Now feeling safe and invincible, he began to rule over the forest. He was fed well and looked after by the other jungle animals.

But one day, one of the banished jackals died, and all the other jackals began to howl. Hearing the howls of the jackals, the blue jackal couldn't help but start howling in response. Since his howls sounded exactly like a jackal, he was soon discovered by the other animals for what he was: a very ordinary jackal! He had been caught red-handed trying to fool them. The animals were furious at this trickery.

Better Safe than Sorry

It is wiser to be cautious and careful than to do something you may regret later.

One day, while crossing a river, a fox got his tail entangled in a bush. He was trapped and couldn't move. Mosquitoes buzzed near the river, and seeing the trapped fox, they descended on him and enjoyed feasting on his blood. The fox could not swish them away since his tail was stuck in the bush. So he had to suffer through the bites.

A hedgehog was strolling by and, seeing the fox's tricky situation, he went up to him. 'How unfortunate this is, my friend,' said the hedgehog. 'Shall I help you by driving off these mosquitoes who are sucking your blood?'

The fox shook his head. 'Thank you, but I would rather you didn't.'

The hedgehog was surprised. 'Why not?' he asked.

The fox replied, 'These mosquitoes have had their fill, and I know they will leave soon. If you drive them away, others will come with their fresh appetite and I may lose more blood. It's better to be safe than sorry.'

Look Before You Leap: Idioms and Phrases from Timeless Tales

Look a Gift Horse in the Mouth

To find fault with something that you have received as a gift.

A long time ago, there was a group of frogs that lived together. But they were unhappy since they had no one to rule them. They decided that they would ask the god of the sky and thunder, Jupiter, to give them a king. Jupiter thought the request was silly, so he threw a log into the pond in which the frogs lived and told them that the log would be their king.

The log made a loud splash as it landed in the water, and the frogs swam away, frightened. At first, the frogs were fearful of their 'king'. And then, when they noticed that the log merely floated silently in the water, they grew more bold and became indifferent to the log.

Soon, they started sitting on the log and gave it little respect.

Thinking that a king like the log was an insult to their dignity, they asked Jupiter to take away the sluggish king and give them another, more suitable one.

Look Before You Leap: Idioms and Phrases from Timeless Tales

Jupiter was annoyed at being pestered once again, so he sent a stork to rule over the frogs. As soon as the stork saw the frogs, he began to catch and eat them.

The frogs who escaped the stork's beak thought, 'We should never have looked a gift horse in the mouth.'

There's No Such Thing as a Free Lunch

Nothing comes for free; there are usually expectations tied to any gift.

There was once a poor but large-hearted man who lived with his wife, Shandili, in a small village. One day, when the sun began its northward journey, the man told his wife, 'Today is an auspicious day. That means people will distribute alms to the poor. I must travel to the next village to see what I can earn. You, too, must find a poor person to feed so that we can celebrate this auspicious occasion.'

Shandili was annoyed. In a raised voice, she said, 'What do you mean by "find a poor person to feed"? We do not even have enough food for ourselves. What should I share? You have kept us poor by giving away everything we have!'

The man was disappointed by his wife's words. 'It is our duty to share what we have,' he said. 'Greed gives us nothing, while sharing even something small will give us the blessings we deserve in this life.' He then went on his way.

Suitably scolded, Shandili decided to check her kitchen for anything she could cook for a poor person. She noticed that she had a small amount of sesame seeds in a container, so she began hulling them by soaking the seeds in warm water so that the husks were easier to remove. She then left the sesame seeds out to dry so that she could cook them once they were no longer damp.

But while the sesame seeds were drying in the sun, a dog came and sniffed and licked the seeds. Shandili was upset, as the purity of her seeds had been compromised. She was not kind. She was cooking for the poor because her husband demanded it of her. She went to her neighbour and offered the husked seeds in exchange for the lady's unhusked seeds. The neighbour was pleased not to have to do the hard work of preparing sesame seeds for cooking, so she was thrilled to make this unusual exchange. But her son, who had been watching the two women, realised the strangeness of this trade and told his mother not to make the swap.

As he led his mother away, the son said, 'If someone offers you something that is better than what you have, and if the gift seems too good to be true, then it's most likely that there is something wrong with it. Remember, there's no such thing as a free lunch!'

To Play With Fire

To take foolish risks without any forethought.

A jackal, on his journey for his next meal, came across two fighting goats in a large clearing. The goats were large and had sharp horns. They were buttressing each other with fierce precision. They were charging at each other and goring each other's skin to establish a victor.

A lot of blood was being spilled as the goats fought. And the jackal, in his greed, licked the few droplets of warm blood that came his way.

'This blood is fresher and better than the blood and flesh of the old animals I am usually able to catch for myself,' he thought.

His greed began to overcome him and he pushed his way between the goats so that he could feast on more blood. As soon as he came close to them, the goats who were angry and in the midst of their fight, gored the greedy jackal to death.

A sage who was walking by observed this and said to himself, 'the foolish jackal should have thought before he jumped. He should have known that if he plays with fire he will get burnt.'

Quality Is Better than Quantity

Sometimes having one item that has been made with great care and expertise is much better than having many items that have been carelessly made and are of a poor standard.

One afternoon, a lioness and a vixen, a female fox, were sunning themselves and talking about their young ones. Like all mothers who are proud of their children, these two were proud of their children. They both talked about how healthy and strong their young were and how shiny their coats were.

The vixen began to brag and said her children were spitting images of their parents. 'My litter of cubs are a joy to see,' she said, and then added maliciously, 'But I notice you only have one.'

'Yes,' said the lioness with a smile, 'but that one's a lion.'

The vixen was left speechless. She realised, 'Quality is better than quantity.'

Look Before You Leap: Idioms and Phrases from Timeless Tales

Many Hands Make Light Work

When everyone pitches in and works together the task at hand becomes much easier to complete.

One day a little sparrow was celebrating the eggs that she had just laid, and the little sparrows that she would soon have in her midst. Suddenly, she felt the shuddering shake of the branch and noticed a crazed elephant hurtling past the tree and knocking the eggs to the ground. Every egg was smashed and her dreams of offsprings were shattered.

The sparrow was distraught and wept loudly. A woodpecker heard her laments and said, 'Life is full of joys and sorrows, my friend. What is the point of this anguish? What you have lost, you have sadly lost forever.'

The sparrow was not comforted by these wise words. She cried even louder and requested that the woodpecker help her avenge the loss of her eggs. 'You must assist me in destroying this thoughtless elephant,' said the sparrow.

The woodpecker thought for a while and said: 'a friend

in need is a friend indeed. Let me see if I can ask my friend the gnat to tell us what to do.' He then flew to gnat and shared the story of the elephant and the sparrow. Gnat buzzed for a bit and spoke: 'I think we may have a solution to this problem. Let me consult with my friend, Frog.'

The frog, gnat and woodpecker came up with a plan. The next afternoon, when it was particularly hot, the gnat flew to the elephant and buzzed loudly in his ear. The elephant was irritated by the sound and began shaking his head. As the elephant continued to be distracted by the buzzing gnat, the woodpecker rushed to his face and pecked out his eyes. The blinded elephant stumbled forward in distress with the buzzing gnat still annoyingly close to his ear. The friends, keeping up the annoying buzz, guided the blind elephant toward the edge of a cliff where the frog sat. The frog began croaking loudly and the sightless elephant thought he was near a watering hole and stepped forward. Sadly, he hurtled down the edge of the cliff and came to an immediate end at the bottom of the pit.

The friends went to the sparrow and said, 'There is nothing that cannot be achieved when friends think ahead and come together. Many hands make light work.'

Look Before You Leap

To consider all possible consequences or dangers before taking any action.

At the end of a long day, a lion who had not found any prey wandered through the forest until he saw a large cave. Though the cave looked like an ideal space for animals to take shelter, it was empty. The lion thought that the cave was most likely occupied by another creature who was away. 'If I hide and wait, the animal will return to the cave at nightfall and can then become my easy prey,' thought the lion. He walked into the cave and hid in the shadows.

In a few hours, a jackal, who lived in the cave, came back home. The jackal noticed that there were paw prints going into the cave, but none coming out. He realised immediately that a lion was waiting for him, but he needed to make sure of this fact before venturing in.

The jackal called out, 'Is anybody there? Cave, may I come in?' There was no answer. So the jackal called out again, 'Cave, you know we have an arrangement and I only come in when you ask me to enter. If you do not reply, I will have to leave and find another cave.'

Hearing these words, the lion immediately said, 'Enter, jackal. It is safe for you to return home. Do come in.' The jackal thus confirmed his suspicions and ran away as fast as he could.

As he escaped, he thought, 'I survived only because I expected danger and acted carefully. I have learnt to look before I leap!'

Author's Note

As the stories from Aesop's Fables and the Panchatantra have shown us, many everyday expressions come from old classical tales. There are, of course, plenty of other sources for idioms that we still use. The great playwright William Shakespeare came up with many of them. In his play *The Merchant of Venice*, the idiom 'a pound of flesh' was used for the first time. This phrase, often used in everyday speech, means extracting a payment or penalty at the expense of something that could cause harm and suffering. The Bible has also given rise to phrases that we use today, like 'a fly in the ointment,' which was first used in the biblical book of *Ecclesiastes*. The phrase means a snag or an irritation that spoils the enjoyment of something.

I have put together some idioms that I use often. I'm certain, they are familiar to you as well. Perhaps you've been using them when you speak? Now that you've rediscovered these quirky phrases called idioms and, in some cases, learnt the origin of many of them, why don't you find stories that illustrate the meaning of these colourful phrases or write some stories yourself? Wouldn't that be a fun exercise?

- **A Penny for Your Thoughts**
  An invitation for people to share their thoughts.

- **Actions Speak Louder Than Words**
  Deeds and actions are more important than mere promises or words.

- **An Arm and a Leg**
  Used to describe something that is very expensive or costs a lot.

- **Back to the Drawing Board**
  Devising a new plan from scratch after the failure of a plan or an idea.

- **The Ball is in Your Court**
  When the responsibility of making a decision or taking action lies with another person

- **Barking Up the Wrong Tree**
  Pursuing a mistaken or unproductive course of action.

- **Beating Around the Bush:**
  To avoid the main topic or be indirect in communication.

IDIOMS IN MUSIC

Here are a few more idioms that you may have encountered and ultilised as well. These are from the vast world of music.

- **Preaching to the Choir**
  Trying to convince people of something they already believe in or are already committed to.

- **Blowing Your Own Trumpet**
  To brag or promote oneself; this gives self-praise a negative connotation.

- **Like a Broken Record**
  To repeat the same thing over and over again, like a scratched or damaged vinyl record that keeps playing the same part.

- **Music to My Ears**
  To hear something pleasing that brings joy or relief.

- **Change Your Tune**
  To alter one's attitude, behaviour or opinion about someone or something.
- **Strikes a Chord**

Something that resonates or evokes strong feelings or memories in a person.

◆ **Singing from the Same Hymn Sheet**
To be in agreement regarding a particular issue or topic.

Appendix

List of Idioms Included in the Book

1. Raining Cats and Dogs
2. Butter Up
3. Head Over Heels
4. Apple of My Eye
5. With Flying Colours
6. Let the Cat Out of the Bag
7. Turn a Blind Eye
8. Under the Weather
9. Spill the Beans
10. Beat around the Bush
11. Every Cloud Has a Silver Lining
12. A Dog in the Manger
13. Necessity Is the Mother of Invention
14. Don't Count Your Chickens before They Hatch
15. Look Before You Leap

16. A Bird in the Hand Is Worth Two in the Bush
17. Honesty Is the Best Policy
18. Slow and Steady Wins the Race
19. Out of the Frying Pan into the Fire
20. Pride Comes before a Fall
21. Sour Grapes
22. Making a Mountain Out of a Molehill
23. Cry Wolf
24. Revenge Is a Double-Edged Sword
25. A Man Is Known by the Company He Keeps
26. Kick a Man When He Is Down
27. The Lion's Share
28. Add Insult to Injury
29. Better Safe than Sorry
30. Look a Gift Horse in the Mouth
31. Quality Is Better than Quantity
32. A Wolf in Sheep's Clothing
33. A Friend in Need Is a Friend Indeed
34. Nothing Ventured, Nothing Gained
35. Look Before You Leap
36. Building Castles in the Air

37. Stick Your Nose into Something
38. Use Your Head
39. Bad Company
40. Snake in the Grass
41. There's No Such Thing as a Free Lunch
42. Fish Out of Water
43. United We Stand, Divided We Fall
44. Bite Off More than You Can Chew
45. Birds of a Feather Flock Together
46. Knowledge Is Power
47. Sly as a Fox
48. As Bold as Brass
49. Like Turkeys Voting for Christmas
50. Turn a Deaf Ear
51. Caught Red-Handed
52. Play with Fire
53. Many Hands Make Light Work

Explore More Idioms and Phrases

We've found that several phrases commonly used today most likely originated from ancient classics, such as *Aesop's Fables* and the *Panchatantra*.

Aesop's Fables is a collection of tales by the Greek slave and storyteller Aesop. Written in Greek in the mid-6th century BCE, these stories were most likely shared orally from person to person, not only to entertain but also to teach morals and lessons.

Historians also suggest that the tales from the *Panchatantra* were most likely composed in the Sanskrit language in 300 BCE. While the original manuscript has yet to endure the test of time, numerous English translations, adaptations and retellings of these age-old stories are now available to the public. The book *Panchatantra* is structured into five (pancha) chapters (tantras), each of which imparts the wisdom of wise conduct and prudent behaviour. Some phrases in these stories are so familiar that they have become part of everyday English.

With 725 Aesop's fables translated into so many languages across the world and over 200 versions of each

Panchatantra narrative available in as many as 50 languages, even people who have never heard of Aesop or his fables or those who have forgotten the Panchatantra tales they heard years back, will recognise many of these expressions.

I suggest you document the idioms and phrases you know of and list new idioms and phrases you come across. Write them down with their meanings in a little booklet and make your own little diary of idioms and phrases.

Other Books by Shobha Tharoor Srinivisan

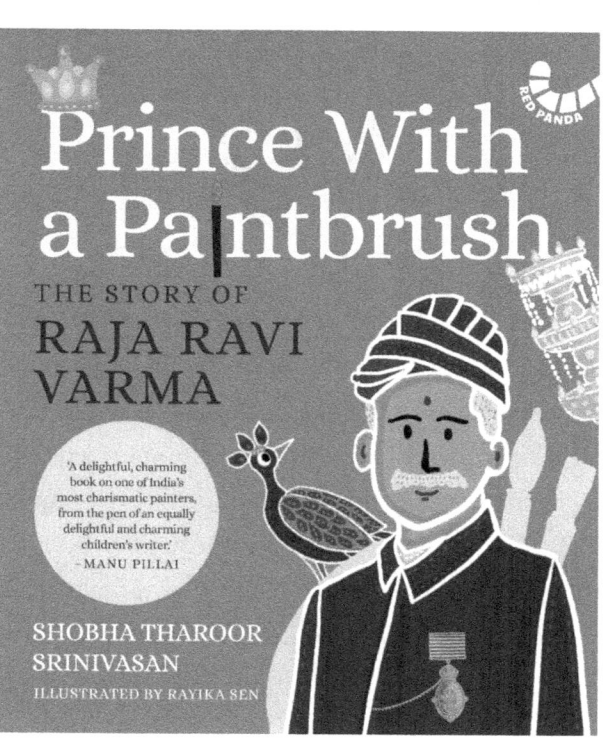

The red panda is a reddish-brown mammal with a long, ringed tail and a raccoon-like face. This endangered animal is found in the forests of eastern Himalayas and is the state animal of Sikkim. Also called firefox, the cat-sized animal is largely herbivores but also eats insects. The red panda uses its bushy tail to balance and wrap it around its body to stay warm in the chilly mountains. A victim of deforestation, there are less than 10,000 animals remaining in the wild.

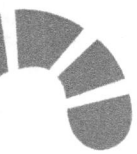

www.ingramcontent.com/pod-product-compliance
Lightning Source LLC
LaVergne TN
LVHW012114070526
838202LV00056B/5731